For Andrew —
Don't read this to
the Kid or his ears
will fall off!
   Love to U-3,
      Bill
      VIII. 12. 75
      NYC

theories of rain
and other poems
bill zavatsky

NEW YORK 1975

A number of these poems have appeared in the following magazines: *Sun, First Issue, Sundial, Columbia Review, Broadway Boogie, Some, Juillard, Eventorium Muse, Milk Quarterly, Roy Rogers, Mulberry, The World.*

Thanks to Leonard Lopate for the lightning

ISBN 0-915342-03-0 (paperback)

ISBN 0-915342-08-1 (hardcover)

Library of Congress Catalog Card No. 74-34537

First Edition

Copyright © 1975 by Bill Zavatsky

SUN publications are edited by Bill Zavatsky from 456 Riverside Drive, New York, N.Y. 10027

To Phyllis

CONTENTS

The Presentation of Self in Everyday Life	3
Aftereffects of the Dance	8
A Preconscious Autobiography	10
To Bill Zavatsky	13
Sleep	15
The Dream	16
Self-Hypnosis	17
The Slave	19
Theories of Rain	20
To Light	28
Kept Awake by Rain	30
Generative	32
Ode	33
You Look Like	35
First Dead Winter Sparrow	36
Too Young to Go Steady	40
Iranistan	41
Seven Twenty Seven Sixty Seven	43
Time	44
Memory	46
To the Pianist Bill Evans	48
Disclosures	51
Rereading Shakespeare	52
Far from the War	54
The Ex-Poet	55
Summer Madness	57
Some Japanese Poems about Roy Rogers	59
My New Year's Literary Resolutions	69

Lessons	75
Testament	76
Goodbye	79
Real Bullets	80

theories of rain
and other poems

The Presentation of Self in Everyday Life

> " . . . I saw the dull yellow eye of the creature open . . . "

I.

Lexicons provoke a kind of madness in me,
Of the quality of too white, too clean sheets.
How many words, like brides, must I lay my head against
Until I can talk again, until I can reach up and seize
A radius of day larger than mind, unlike the clown
Shot and bandaged on the floor of my father's face?

Once vocabulary worn in snow dissolved
The cloud banks for me, dispensing glows that made
My head less ill. Now
Past gold and frankincense and myrrh
Is it better to retain the glossary of anxiety,
Like a fistfull of paper money
soaked with gasoline and fumes, kinetic, than to isolate
A Frankensteinian talent for blades and swift reprisals?

II.

Mommy and daddy grew frightened.
They would not see their son
Becoming the dentist of nerves . . .
To tear out his nerves and slide them beneath their pillow
To hide the mother and father beneath my breath
As God is hidden beneath the tongue
Speaking from the bloody dream around my bed,
Its roots dragging my face, then to sleep at last
Slowly falling toward Spring

They were so frightened, grown
So used to doing none of the talking.
Can't somebody make this thing we made shut up?

III.

My blood shot into a girl
Being lashed with roses.
I signed for a transfusion of skills
Which saw me more in pieces the more I saw.
At first I loved Electricity in my arms.
It took me years to place the burning smell.
I tore the electrodes away
And do I shine?—Much like the skulls of my age!

I crushed the lenses full of my baby life.
From feelings I fit new spectacles to my face
Then plotted the map of my sight
From relative hates.
I stumbled through the landscape striking matches.
High tension wired me with bad lies,
Denied me the circuits of angelic lips
And their friends, our lonely fingers and hands,
Magic beasts that are helpless and almost blind
Leaping back from the claws of other children.
Words, stop me from shining like the clarity
Of explanation; rest my lips close
To the bloodfilled edges of the clearly seen.

IV.

Not enough to describe the dancing mother who screams
At her son-in-a-cloud with a bamboo handle
Pressed in his cheek, lawn pungent with broken grass.
Not enough that images race past the pylons of breath,
Crash together in the air; that molecular smoke
Drift against the faces of the departing crowd.
Fresh conclusions assemble their model of pain
Like leaves run backwards from Autumn to Spring
Through the block where the boy grew up,

The projector of light.
                        He was the thing
Assembled under the darkened Christmas tree.

His father's silver tools and smudges
Crashed in his forehead like cosmetics
Of the future perfect. *In the future* he thought
I will be perfect, I'll land atop a rock and speak.
Swarms of fetuses (the child's interior monologues)
Lit up his inkwell at school, then advanced
To a square and to this day may be seen laughing
About a youth who is making speeches in white,
Disguised as a man with nothing but purity,
No other past than snow. We know
How this child defeated the ice and snow. They know
The mad mechanic who gave him life,
The partnerless dancer who wanted him
To dance. That's why they laugh

V.

Here I stand, the only child
Who knows the meaning of *prestidigitation*
In a world of adult technicians.
Shall I reveal it?
My fingers speed through their words
My hands are the medium of another world
Slowly wiping them out
On the black and white surfaces.
They thought they taught me the accordion:
With several adjustments, I aimed the Death Ray
     machine.

Torn Houdini posters everywhere,
My pal's blue jaw hooked by a horrible premise—
The coffin : a dazzling grid,

An equation spanning a freak ventriloquism—
The stupidity of memory,
Of music sanded, inlaid with every hair and nail
Of human ambition:
The art of playing accordion in a coffin
The art of throwing passes from the tomb.
Where the combed hairs of his hands
Pushed a path through the universe
I walked on to my room
Where he waited for me, lying on my bed
In cones of light, who
Walked me to school when I was small
Who punished me when I ran fast
But this was his greatest lesson.

Shreds of Houdini on the electric pole
Houdini hanging from the Giant Market wall,
Roof ripply with glassy clouds, defunct cereals
Screaming in our green shopping cart.
A hand was holding me back
But I looked through his glowing eyes!
Evidence of Houdini, pieces everywhere,
Giant among the expressions of dead grains

VI.

I see this girl.
When I touch her, why, I change!
Even razors hate their cutting business.
What else was I trained to do?
My cathedral flares
With sun and cinders,
Afflicting her legs with a sheer aurora.
In the translation I avoid
I am a siren in use as a dream
Grinding glass through air.

I never believed in these jars of the specimen "Light"
I never wanted the fevers, first Rough, then Smooth
Turning into wood in a world of nails and saws!
Carefully how I had to breathe and lie
Or the stitches would explode
Or nothing in me could ever fit together . . .

VII.

High above town in my own lab
I don't care what anybody thinks.
I adore what I make—these images,
These freaks.
Whatever my feelings say
My monsters kiss and dance.

To you, ugliness hanging in the mirror,
I oppose my few powers.
In my fist I flash up angels at you,
Hack at you with my mouth.
Words are not sorry
The houses that they live in for a minute
In the brain
Must be burned to the ground
In the service of fresh beauty.

My commotions
Are wrapped in blue stems,
In rain, shaking.
In flashes of lightning, colossal in the moonlight

As the villagers approach my tower
With their clubs and their torches

Aftereffects of the Dance

I'm back. Though the moon
exhausted my nostrils with sugar.
Experience likes my body, sky
preparing darkness with a spoon
for my body, holding a testicle
of glass and a paper ovary.

I was born when the wind lifted
its golden megaphone. Writing
scribbled the inner walls of my temples.
I discovered sunset isn't a knife at my throat
that clouds do not conceal embalmed angels
that I have people to see behind the light.

I light cigarettes to honor the stars.
Feeling brightness my nerves trace and cut
wings and shadows from the air.
Rabbits eat the heads off tulips every year.
Heartbeats grace the branchends of a tree
and every year, for months, petals detain me:
importance to be attached.

Dancing more, more of me
occurs between branch and floor—
April raising its face from the ice,
its radical ideology. Like tractors
lining the soft wings of a hen, rain
sings as it speeds toward human throats,

In hope of beading near what does the singing.
The dance is over. Through it the clock
was a bird with matches for wings.
And through the long night I rub the air so much
I run out of hands—though I can sing!

Though no one will love these songs for years . . .

And when I sing my breath can rip a January wind
and pour its chestbones in a cup.
Stopsigns collapse into screams that materialize
cars. Not the swan, the dream of the swan
and the luminous garden water: I sing
for the beautiful daughter of communist troops,
blue eyelike saw against idiot laughter.

Larvae sleep, tier after tier, in the mine
this eye discovers around leaves; what a tree
sees with, moment to moment, by falling.
Then bugs are crashing lids, they want to be
what I invent when I tell you
what you mean to me as I watch you dance.

I seek the rind of imagining galaxies
in the pores of my face, in the air
with its priceless violin. An orange
receives my fingers in the mail. Wind
scrapes its binoculars on the geology
I am hanging note by note in the air,
the only way I can climb inside heaven.

I am a steeple of blood with a throat
and demolish the register when I scream
of love and punishment and youth and gold.
I am your only son, who does not dance,
who plays the music for the dance. Who
sleeps too much because there is this face,
there is this other tree moving in the world
shedding brightness its activity

A Preconscious Autobiography

Once I grew up to an age
where a dead green president
almost drafted me,
tension nearly mutilated me.
When a packet of matches destroyed
the supernatural collar that pursued me,
I abandoned a monumental quest
through the vistas and official sites
of the dollar bill. Pale gravure,
you leaned vert ornamental lips
out of gelid margins to me
and spoke a scrapy dental speech
about the thrills of loot.
You sweated to fashion a filter
to fit my ear—to pipe your tender smoke through:
the dead symmetrical language of the circle.
But doped up for this spectacle
and guided in silent carriages
crawling along to a saint or a school,
I stumbled on a distinct sound.
In my confinement rested a blue urn,
the only urn I've ever understood.
Inside this vast urn I knocked over
the penny of scorching ice, the payment
on Shelley and Keats' eyes, the city atlas
of Mayakovsky's skull shaved whiter than snowbells
blaring their Georgian Russian light,
O scalp so bright displaced by my father's brothers!
These creepy relations won't lend me four bones
to patch up my damaged marimba plantation
or revamp the new lobe of my sun . . .
It's a shame their Second World War for Souvenirs
is over—my war's just becoming fun.

I'm fixing up my Zero to fly against them,
I desire their toothy wallets in my Kyoto den!
As I say—to buy the zircons I deplete
(practicing standing in twilight like a lamp)
I got work as a sullen acrobat
leaping and squeezing the accordion
at the outskirts of my pain
which nightly I am compensating
by leaning terribly toward the moon,
moon intent on the blue suicide of dawn!
I failed because the accordion
is a limited sexual instrument, failed
when my hands could not wed my ear
to the Polka of Polish Management.
Next I tried for political asylum,
applying to the pink Madagascan chieftain
who ruled the first postal domain I collected.
He said "Go away you son of a factory!"
which in the translation I avoid I am.
To try to transcend such roots
I sought the Reality Principle Scholarship
at First Choice University but was turned down
much as a red plaid cap in winter
with gruesome earlaps is, in a boy's anthology of hats.
Tearing open the envelope like an avalanche, I was
 crushed.
Soon I was doing a stint converting burps
into epic histories of: *Herrings, Their Destruction
and Redemption*, focussing on three inches
of large intestine little fishes
really feel at home in. I asked questions
of the Nile:
    "How does it go with you, River?"
    "Doesn't your pelvis get sore?"
"Are your ripples a kind of escalation of rhyme?"
And "Is that an organ beneath your wavy hair?"

Finally I lost the nerve to retell this story.
One night I fell asleep inside my history
and couldn't climb down so much
I had to laugh. Still clutching my sound like a bike
ground, or Saint Relica her ear,
I woke up on an island run by friendly bees.
I write much of the wind for the island,
and in my poems make notes toward occasional rain.
You should hear the incredible yellow hum
and taste the delicious bee-ade I wash down
with tiny golden cakes. And the bee-folk tell me
you are flying here!

To Bill Zavatsky

He must learn not to neglect
What comes out of my mouth.
Don't ever forget what it's like
When you're the musician, either

You must unstrap the gold bonnet sometime,
Lifting over his head
These several figures of speech.

These figures move like the animals
Tattooed on the band of the bonnet.
They don't go to sleep.
They lick themselves and keep you awake
When your head should be sleeping

Bill, set the bonnet on my desk
Like a nylon wig. Remember there are entities
So compact in their being they must be singing.
Now you are in for a very human experience

Forget imitating the rain.
Instead, and nightly, go freeing the flags from the
    matches.
Delete the apocalyptical Indian on the local lawn,
Right out of Blake, wearing the American flag.
Or think of him constantly, but
Note well: That redskin is full of mischief.

Remember there is the condensation
And the speed.
Flak crowning a dark bomber in flight
Isn't the way you think, so forget it
To absorb a number of influences, the tree

In the rainy garden. To approximate a music
So intense it's releasing forgotten colors
Go to the lake.
Wire your arm to the lake
And write: a clear poetic.
Bill, you must learn to be amused
By one just lovely thing

There are sails buried in the rain.
Your stanzas are shaped like sails.
Learn to use the craft and the edge of the water

At sea in the right little boat
Climb up the wood to the stars
And rub your hands against the blue glass.
Then take your lips and kiss,
Bill, and whisper
"Nancy and Sluggo come closer"
"Vergil and Dante come closer"

If you don't hear a thing
If you have been very successful
I may be asleep

Sleep

    A person sleeps, is beautiful

       beyond its punctuation

          as if

    she floated above himself

into space where they cannot fall

      by speech or breath

The Dream

Now I feel my death so near
I can't smash in this door

In the world that starts like an engine beyond
The blade of vision, my Angel struts:
The frame, the skeleton of last night's dream,
An aircraft of great wings
And bones, waiting. Fabric
Hacked away by blue axes the air holds
Made tailspins happen with a vengeance—
As when slate colonial tombstones
Like the sculpted angels that plan allegory
Fly upright into funereal Connecticut landscape:
Trees toss flowers and leaves lose—
Reds, violets, greens pale, rot, and collapse
Like the airliner's lights driven in the granite mountain
And the ground is untouched.

How much horror can a door contain?
Lift the hood to reveal the corpse
That has been your engine; that has driven
The pink American machine you love to exhibit

This is how the Angel defined the dimensions
The falling structure of the dream
As he held my skull like light in his hollow hands
And spoke distinctly, face pressed into mine

Self-Hypnosis

You are going into a deep sleep.
Deep.
Very deep.

> You will attract women . . .
> and horses.
> You will get cabs . . .
> as no other human before.
> These cabs will skid to your feet
> like grounders. Like flowers
> flashing toward you
> in the ghastly rush-hour light . . .
> You will realize . . .
> there is nothing more beautiful
> than someone hailing a cab.
> And you will bear the Perfume . . .
> the Perfume of Immorality,
> concocted

>> of one part ostrich lisp
>> of a deaf ear whispered full
>>   of immortal suggestions
>> made from the stamp of demented
>>   postal chiefs, in Arizona!
>> two knobs from the broken guitar
>>   of a rock 'n' roll star
>> brewed with a Babe Ruth candy bar
>>   tenderized by a train
>> of livid bat spit and Commie come
>> and mingled with every OF in your
>>   vicinity . . . the parachute
>>   worlds this word unfolds . . .

You will fly in this peculiar odor
through the night . . .
and now and then you will whinny!
And women will think it's funny and
    fall backwards
I will be waiting for you around the corner . . .
where you will bring them to meet me!

And now, as I count to three . . .
you will awaken . . .
And you will remember nothing of what I have told you

The Slave

Hand
I want you to write a poem
to yourself
all by yourself

Rush to your corner
and change into my desires

And when you are dressed so perfectly
you can't stand playing the puppet
of my terrified body

Plunge yourself through the merciless world
like a pencil
Scribble a path out of this world
and up among the stars
hang like a trowel

Descend to your place beside the sleeves
of waves
and push some of their brightness
toward this page

Dance back into the skies
like a bird
that closes its eyes
as it flaps in its cage
and sings
I shall always have wings!

Theories of Rain

to Kenneth Koch

If it rains in this poem
Then that's a fine rain, sweet rain, pretty girl!
O beau and belle pluie, you've legs of your own . . .
Jump down and crouch here, anoint my feet Light Rain,
Where Rain I can't load my capsules, blue words
To prescribe your dosage for my ravenous azure
    vocabulary.
Doctor Nurse Rain, you've rummaged around my duds so
    frequently—
Continually revived on the cloudy ambulance of your
    knockout drops
By pungent snorts of the color bows tied in your hair,
Clear salts, crystals of an all-weather charity.
I am no flooded attic bayonet, no Korean symbol
    immersed in the subconscious
Of a cardboard trunk, no crucifix nailed
To the inevitable tinder of my ancestors' dopey
    proclivities
The way you seem . . . but aren't we both astonished
When an eggish hail smashes from our outspread wings,
Hysterically flagging and boarding the vehicles of a
    pleasant shower
That suddenly pummel blood from a gay feathered hat?
And can we face our traffic's senseless atavism?
    Ashamed?
Brutishly scaring the daylights with our emotional fads,
Uncontrollable, crushing the umbrella's perfectly
    heartshaped ass?
Yet the possible intrusion of an elaborate hollow jewelry,
And snow a chill confetti mixture of self-celebration,
    cerebration?
Rain please leave me alone . . . water, cease to evaporate
From my brains. Air in my mind, do not carry the

      transparent and invisible vapor of thought.
Process unknown to me or to anyone living or dead,
    refuse
To think and cool and abstract and rise in the atmosphere
    of my hair.
Visible formal clouds, images, refrain from singing the
    song
About saturation and beyond. Images, hinder your
    growth, your particles, abstain from dancing in
    lightning,
From becoming my heart, so potent, so precipitous, do
    not fall back to my brow
In the shape of a verb, a drizzle of bead . . .

A wind rose confabulated of a lot of the water in the air,
The frightened weather map hair!
                                     See, I'd even compare thee
To the astrolabe, if only I knew what that was . . .
Rain, please get out of my system . . .
                                        See that Fire Door?
(Oops, I've directed the Rain off a cliff!) Oh tincture
    condensers,
Porcelain sparkplugs, brittle farts,
Broken open the black rocks pretend that you are the
    yolk of the sea!
O hallucinatory testicles and breasts, O diamond zinnia
    articles
Boffing stamp collections of a tree pianoforte,
Microcosms of *to be*: "is" "was" "am" WHAM!
The Fire Door slams shut.
                        Not little pillow left for ant
To lay his weary hat.
                    But O free doggy pub!
O downcast moorish pinnacle smidgens, O giant accident
    glass
Ah silent arterial beans! O rarebits of white icicle

Banging around inside a girl's thigh bluejean . . .
Wow medicine hat, argh lively prune, sieve, apple angels,
Whiz Gothic drum and rutabaga delirium tremens, O
    comparable to duck smut!
Lo spaceships, don't stop invading the windshields, the
    disgruntled pup, O water pistol blatt!
Or blipping signals from the neutrons of Claremont
    Avenue . . .

Blind rain, rain slaw, and rain bugle
And rain theremin that scared us half in half and rain iota
Buffalo escadrille rain and the gearstripping rain of the
    chords, of the clouds
The lethal freckle rain that bumped off so many
Occult and amulet neon rain, the Peach Map
    Expeditionary Rain
The sunlight utensils and Ear Market rain, the lost Rain
    Unit
And the atomic radiation over Utah snow the sheep
    munched
And the architecturally sound rain, the bebop rain of the
    rainorootie and oo-bop-sh'bam rain
And the tepee sex-party rain that got us unsnapping our
    habiliments
And the adjustable indoor rainstorm kit, with hot & cold
    showers that condense little fog-drops on the
    window in a paradigm of the atmospheric cough of
    the rain phenomenon
And the glove compartment rain that soaked the car thief
    because our dash plugs right in a yellow hydrant
And the final examination rain of blood and terror
Rain fingering the heads at the Insane Farm picnic lunch
And the cancelled Soldiers & Sailors poetry reading rain
    and only the luminous steps and a pigeon and I have
    come to listen to the Rain intone all its latest poems
And the awkward young girl rain half-dumb and

      -understanding of its own beauty as it gropes on
      Broadway for a contact lens that sparkles, adrift on
      the eyeball of a puddle.
And the inverse negative capability rain of Berkeley
      California that fails to dent Phillip's wild black hair
And the famous and dear Roy Rogers rain, so the King of
      the Cowboys and Dale halt their ponies and yodel
The Buddy Holly rain that even in death drifts through
      his pure voice, the tenebrous voice of the Robert
      Desnos rain that has mantled the concentration
      camp poles, that has modified all the flowers and
      blows through my own timorous voice
In the silent voice of Fantômas, a black rain
And the Frank O'Hara cloudburst, that clears away death
      by greeting its sundry manifestations of sex,
      adolescent pustules and boners, by a clear
      integration love permits only the genuinely fragile
      great
The immense Desnos Eluard and Reverdy rain of voices
      composing all of our lips aloft over a sample
      Olivetti, punching freely away at the stars, like you
      at our backs Rain . . .

    When I ponder the Red Communist rain, and the
          skunk pink
    Baudelairean rain, and the exacting historical
          Trotskyite
    Rainlike mechanism falling on poets everywhere like
          a snow
    Spun out of china, smacking their shoulder blades
          and knuckles,
    And which they shake off like horses continuing to
          the light,
    And the quiescent Academy of American Poets rain,
          and the vintage
    Parisian rainfall, and the LSD Hippie rain—quick, tilt up

>   Your mouth!—and all the rainfall products in books
>   and movies,
>   The antique *Atlantic Monthly* rain . . .
>   You are not
> Just under my skin or in my shoes or never far away from
>   me
> Singing or tapdancing, spoons clacking vertiginously
>   inside my bumbershoot—
> You are the moonshine tomato cans remember, and
>   nothing more . . .
> A water cup balanced on a sill yellow sunshine is racing
>   for,
> And I tremble at your potency, which is my own,
> To be shocked a Monday at what's all over my shoes,
> Wednesday only a dull streak on the curb, and by Friday
> A clean and virile rain has erased all my notions of Art,
> Which remains just a person's name, I aspire to meet him!
> Someone remarkably similar to myself—and I think it *is*
>   me!
>
> But I am only a toy of the Wind and the Rain, a balsa
>   fighter.
> I am a citizen of the state of water vapor in the air,
> The politics of the density of air impel me.
> I am a square of cement, Rain. Not so fast! And not in
>   French.
> I figured, No, I'd never write of you, but
> How you flashed like headlights through my canebrake
>   locks!
> Then borrowed my ballpoint (your slovenly penmanship!)
> Or collided with my keys, Lightsome Typist!
>   "Beware"
> You announce to the trees, "A Major Poet is in your mist . . ."
> Leafy jump kit cables blast us into your prosody-like sky,
> If it ever gets started raining, if it's any good . . .
> Your song at its best: the "intimately lived with" lines.

Your dress: a translation who never betrays my dreams
Of a nude swimming elephant water poetess!
Out in you, I get a feeling illegal cargo imbues my body,
    Rain.
Do you think you're a cop? You,
In possession of all the most dangerous drugs!
You act like air force birdbath delinquency, minutes
    around
The bottleneck, Superman dunking the secret polar bomb
    orchid
Thus collapsing the Eskimo mad philosopher plot—
A theorem blowout at 75, a mud puddle resolution
Or a conclusion enlisting the widest bluest eyed navy . . .

Once the process of rain faltered in my head
When you and I snagged the fin of darkly beautiful
Watery night where the current of my hands disclosed
    itself
"As often many in the art of rain . . ."
I permitted to slip away. The lost half of the night
(Was this also you?) outside my window, pouring.
To imitate how you fill my dreams with what you were
    up to then
I wrote "As often many in the art of rain" again,
Urging atmospheric turbulence to thunder inside my pen,
Releasing my words like unnavigable sums to climb to her
    room
Love splashing our mouths and our thighs caught up
In the arms of it, the gentle rainy terms of it . . .

Rain, you have hoodwinked those tyrants, "like" and "as"—
"You fall like," "You plummet as": cantankerous dull
    grey brains, housings supple with lightning
That open their bomb bay doors, and the poets and
    weathermen
Illuminated beneath great cumbersome umbrellas fume

At the collective idiocy of their publications and drip with
    revisions!
We are dumbbells you exercise in the night! We are stupid
    ambassadors hijacked pants-down in flight, colonials
    stabbed by a parrot revolutionary fever—
For a moment exulting, soaked with the blood of the
    absolutely free . . .
The fabulous blood of you and me . . .
Still some flecks of you veer, Rain, and orbit my pencil.
But Rain you aren't rhetorical, easily dismantled,
    chromium hubcap,
Though you gesture, though you repeat the bough of
    yourself, a connective, a driveshaft
Of gossip, a cluster of orange berries the light can see
    through
Into the innards that detain and collate light every
    whichway,
As in the water glass machine. And also you are red, and
    hold,
And impersonate the light, dangling from little trees
Those birds her eyes glide to and yank its blue labels . . .
I prowl, I slip under your hem, I am hypnotized
With the trees, all ears for white thumbnail shrieks
The college campus reverberates, seized by raindrops!
Clear cockpits as pilotless as leaves, river and cockpit tear—
Federico Lorca's airship parked by the sidewalk . . .
O "disremember" superior to "forget"!
O April lessons, lesions, and furniture!
Excessive musical toots, the boy-copied pointers that
    tortured my youth of pimples—not wood!
Unregretted and undisremembered, capgun tonalities,
    flora & fauna and Nina!
Why you're the unmetronomed Princess with Perfect
    Time!
Why you are the one who pinned the white links to my
    shirt,

And the cufflinks that fasten my hands through space
    and rhyme
In your silent fashion—
Why you combined in the web no sunshine guns can
    penetrate!
This glove, this reality, Rain, these brooches of an
    ultimate fiction
In my future. Rain, I accept you, I breathe in the
    downpour

To Light

I have built the rain,
alone in my room.

Now if I design the rain another voice
O shadow, O light
who will walk in and scream at me?

Whose voice shall I turn to
for a model in a thousand songs?

My tendency would be to leave you now,
Light, a little in the dark,
and sleep to gain release from your impossible
    maintenance.

Fold me, yes,
don't leave me lying here
like a baseball lost in the grass.
Don't make me writhe around
like a bone in the Great Plains of moonlight
clawing for a socket.

Suddenly you flash on in my brain,
Bones and Moonlight!
The possibility of a monstrous ode to you.
I am no forest at night when clouds
lower their white anchors slowly, scraping the leaves.
Only the rain-forest of prehistory
hammered into charcoal pebbles
by the square feet of our fathers
could write your ode, O Bones, O Moonlight!

Yet I could be so pure . . .
Didn't I go to school day after day in the air?
I can't stop singing the melody of the bee, bee
who strikes the shining fenders of flowers by day,
by red, by blue, by glowing velvet nozzles . . .
Your melody coaxed from me like true honey,
The honey crushing memory from the tongue.

I refuse to be ignored
in my grey world, like a spent bulb.
Lightning, write me into your will—
as if every shining species couldn't get along without me
as if every singing species knew me by heart.
I will supply the shadow part. My words nail out a night
your scissors tear in two,
moving along the sky immense as sight.
O Immense-as-Bright
I live in this darkened shed until you come,
I sing to you.

Kept Awake by Rain

Each raindrop
slaps the heart
like a typewriter
key: the spindle
revolves, a city
heart, bruised by traffic
like raindrops
crushed on chrome

fingers flashing
an Egypt of rings,
which circle and choose
this morning to build
monuments to human hands

Pressures adjusting
my temples
with odd ticking:
song words   eggs
tapped across iron airshafts,
the heartbeat of glass
under siege

the clash of atoms
in air-conditioner housings,
the velvet stacks
of a tug
        fraying

from leaf to
leaf, from cloud
to river
up to its lips
in darkness

another flying drop
another word
another line

cut from the whiteness of dawn

Generative

To make
of fatigue
what's fresh
as the space
between boughs,

like animal claws
crusted with ice,
steaming, fixed where autumn
stained them, as attitudes

we have never thought to question
however bent or unfinished they departed
us, displayed in that humdrum instant
we are re-realizingly continuing
and refracting, Januarily:
habitual stance, impressions real

if not so clear and cold
as the ice curves, demanding
us to notice us, where
they were sending us,
pestering and urging us
to come, and coming alive
within those hiatuses

Ode

    Your door. You gold.
    You most excellent.
    How can you take me in and wet me and push me back unharmed?
    How did I go in you and feel and never relinquish that feeling or you?

    Do you sleep? Am I in your dream?
    Am I closer to sleep, in you?
    Closer to what has taken a breath and held it?
    And in that bubble of breath do I splash and laugh?
    Are my fingernails of foam?

    I remember the Elastic World I came from.
    I jam my eyes on my little fists and strain . . .
    I can remember until I am fluid completely deathless!
    You air.
    Letting me finger you letting me dash my hands in you.
    For when you surround us our bodies appear to be singing smashing across the gold network of dawn by shaking its striations and hard lampnesses in the face of the pool.
    Beginning to smile faintly packaged in a wave beginning to be torn open eagerly by hands beginning to move the jaw beginning the being of moving with it and finally delivery itself, the gold fire water air song of a branch in flames on a darkened lake!

    I am moving the ocean in my arms, sharing me like a brother kissing me like a sister telling me like a father giving me like a mother to shore after shore, finger upon lip,

Like a tribe! A navy of hands!
How much you want me!
Why else would you permit me touching a woman where she portrays you so I may possess the gift of plunging up to my hair in the mirror again and again where light escapes through the lines and cracks of the body and flows around the elements that test us,
Entering us as apples lifted by trees which swim through their own classical solutions, the leaves navigating the air, deadly and luminous, like us.

You god.
The ripples in my face: reflection, breath: beginning to move

You Look Like

to Phyllis

You look like Sappho giving a reading
You look like what Sappho said dying
Sappho who did not look at all like Gertrude Stein

You look like those Queens of the Adjectives the flowers
You look like me the hours I waited the summer
I waited for you so much I was you
Eyelids streaked with Mediterranean powders

How you step in a room naked where I am sleeping—
As if I were doing important sleeping!

And you—*you shine the morning off you*—
Like the fragrant island sunlight Sappho knew

First Dead Winter Sparrow

Gee
did you drop from the sky
to the pavement
116th and Riverside?

I bet someone
is missing you, you
are so taut,
like a window shade

curled in a school
and leaking that precocious
winter light
with chills

for your dead
feathers
and mine that live

You will be squashed
by an immense
tire

on the muddy
undercarriage
the tire supports,

which isn't Spring

The literature of dead
animals
disgusts me,
as you

When I was big
as you
I fawned
over a sob

I took all tiny
pictorial beasts
to heart

This heart
pulls the strings
on my soupy
emotional life

Evanescent forms
go out
in the trash

I knew a lake
a cousin
filled with wings

Are my emotions
elderly? I
will feed you

Is death my
friend? You
will seed me

In elementary school
a boy was famous

He was the boy
when cats were found
from clotheslines

He was the boy
who invented the
miniature gallows

the ingenious device

the inverted handle
of a trash can lid

He was the boy
who liked
to beat people up, sparrow

were you beat up
by the wind?
I know

the confusion
of the sky
I know how often

I mistake
the cement
for the sky
the glass for air

You are not
a cartoon bird

You will not rise
from the dead

If I find you
in the pages
of a book

I cannot imitate
your sound,
a flower of paper

Or do you exist
to adorn my world?

You would seem funny
to my lapel

I am no monster though

I am an animal too

Doing all the animal
can do
I notice you
by the curb

Too Young To Go Steady

My ear was damaged on a little walk
To school. To school! And in a talk
Of crime rate Fred broke my nose, Fred
Who's dynamited split-levels in Marilyn
And is licensed to kill with his hand!
    Song: Please don't press me
                I'm afraid you'll crush me
A song of a rose you buried in a book
Of the Rossetti girl is still burning
While trying to smell its folded body
To see if it's alive a little.
And are you worried any in the street
When we put letters to Spain in the fireman's hat
And do they get there? Does Lorca open mail
With the soft Andalusian verb behind his hair
Like a yellow eagle? Not that U.S. bird, but a flyer
All astral hat and derangement goggles
Who soars like Rocket Man on giant ears
Damaged on the way to school. Its bricks
Are beaten out of blood and light,
Light we go swimming in that's never let in
Through the leaden goggles of the window shields
Wrapped around the head of the school.
We live in Fuddville, the city with the bridge
That killed herself. One night she unstrapped
Her belt of blue lights, she didn't wave,
She leaped off her feet through the bay.
We children saw and turned our backs
On our teachers for Mission soda
And a government of drugs

Iranistan

Iranistan: or, my grandmother's interpretation—an invented brave gasping to the council "*I ran* and now *I stand*"; for the mission (which was his message) balanced the fate of the tribe and the gods, and here is another web she drew from her white hair the way I had always known her to endorse myth, the lamplight fusing into the corner we waited (at Water and Fairfield) for the Gray Line Bus to swoop and hiss and carry us on its thin orange arrow to Iranistan where we lived at Hanover.

Mother, the lamplight's explaining the facts of life to me! Mother, is this voice yours? The one talking me into the air, amazed that mild autumn evening at what you (*is this you?*) are telling me of bodies and feeling and love and how beautiful it was to you as we stand on our feet for the Gray Line Bus that moves down Fairfield slowly, turning left at Iranistan always, toward the mansion of Phineas T. Barnum destroyed by fire, "Iranistan," ghostly on the lawns above the Sound.

Barnum inspects the sea from his metal chair. Sea that never fails to be the circus he thinks. His neighbor Elias Howe, within barking distance, cradles the original sewing machine and the name of my school beginning in his green arms,
    Sewing machine that is plunging through the sea, worked by the foot!

            and *odi persicos* I read
              odi persicos
                      but Iranistan!

Iranistan as I saw it this afternoon, seen from that

evening: the lamplight swarming with facts as I eagerly went through the book of erotic pictures from the East in the bookstore, how they curved in love and the shapes of love they formed

Iranistan. Oriental villa

Seven Twenty Seven Sixty Seven

For a moment I thought, That's *you* crossing the street!
That terribly long tall beautiful girl . . .
Does anyone know her, her name or what she does?
Anyhow,
          There she goes.

Time

B.R.

Knew you were in the city
Every edition of the phonebook
I still look you up, sometimes twice

You would call me at school
I would pretend to be cut off
You curse—I am lost—I hear you

Found your letter from the summer
you invited me—"Come everyweekend!"
A squashed bug circled on the envelope

"We have signals worked out" you said
(You and the family you stayed with)
"And they'll leave us alone if I do *this*"

Eight years! How you jumped up
at the reading: "Just got my period!"
I think of your unsurpassable body

Marching with the Communist Youth
The new mystery of the peace sign on your wall
But I was afraid to attend their party with you

Maybe studying botany now I remember
Your special plan, so eager for books again,
having made love astonishingly

Do you hide in the phonebook under another man?
You simply weren't the kind of girl one marries
(I wrote that didn't I)

It is still impossible for me to speak
clearly and wasn't I also the one
who made you ashamed of what you had written

And am I the one who dreams of you
on a commune with a black man a waitress
a junkie a topless dancer a floating corpse?

"All I want to do is come and be naked with you"
I hear you speaking from 1965
And in your memory I touch my body

Memory

Why now? This time of year? Summer
When you bought a present in the bookstore
and I ran to catch you, ran shouting "Miss!
Miss!" as if there was something you had left.

When you walked out the door I couldn't stand
to think you would forget me, felt
forgotten that very moment, ten years later
I am still out of breath trying to catch

what the body remembers, what the mind rejects.

The sun is up and filling in the blind.
The cat walks in, and stops, and watches me
scribble, eyes clicking like a digital clock.

The last time I saw you, in dayglo green,
you were rushing up the street to catch the train.

By the time your face whipped by like an express,
yelling was no use.
You'd changed. I had changed.
My hair was long, I had married,
was teaching school

>   *Mr. Bill*
>   *He use to be so cool*
>   *but now he a fool*

The faces of children I've loved
The ones who drove me crazy
Rapid transit.
Cabs yellow as speeding morning air.

Smoke another cigar.

Tell me where all lost things are
July 1974

Unruly sun

To the Pianist Bill Evans

When I hear you
play "My Foolish Heart"
I am clouded

remembering more than
Scott LaFaro's charred bass
as it rested

against a Yonkers wall
in its transit
from accidental fire

like a shadowy
grace note
exploding into

rhythms of Lou
insanely driving
"Man, we're *late*!"

his long curved bass
straining the car
interior, a canvas swan

my hand clutched,
fingered, refingered:
steel strings as

of the human neck
the vulnerable neck
the neck of music

squeezed by hands
the fragile box
of song, the breath

I crushed out of music
before I killed
by accident

whatever in me
could sing
not touching the keyboard

of terrible parties
and snow
        snow

falling as canvas and
wood and hair flamed
behind a windshield

I imagined being
trapped inside, still
see it in my heart

our terror magnified
note by note
purified each year

the gentle rise
and circle of
cinders in

February air
in their transit
from fire

into music,
into memory, a space
where heroin

does not slowly wave
its blazing arm,
like smoking ivory

teeth and fingers
scorched by the
proximity

of cigarettes laid
on anonymous piano
lips that crush

our function, in-
transigent wire,
inanimate wood

of another century
we must save by song!
for which we are paid!

continuing to be
used, insisting
our hands present

themselves
and keep
on taking our hands

Disclosures

At my father's house in Connecticut: no one home
But a wasp I hear and see and rush to spray.
Several miles away my mother shapes pockets
For blades in an aircraft factory. She lives alone.

Pot-pan noise drifts out to me, sound spoons me
Up its meal of preparation from beneath the newest wing
Of Ed's nice home nextdoor, and Ed is home. I am
     hungry.

From my chair on this screened-in porch I love
So much, I see his younger son lifting a power tool
In bluejeans and white teeshirt. The bell
In one of the Protestant steeples calls for what
This overcast Saturday afternoon? A cobweb trembles
Lightly where brick and wood hold the screen,
A wave sectioned by breeze, protecting a nest
Of wasps, neither out of house nor in.

Spoons knock on wood. Nails shower into jars.
A good meal sniffs its way to me. The scuff of chairs
From nextdoor Ed's, who shows his boys how.
My father let me rake; machinery run on gasoline
Is his specialty. I would only hurt myself.

No wasp noise now. All the trees do is grow.
A froth of Raid clings to the screen, technological semen.

Here one comes again—for what? To fly to death?
To play the survivor of a ruined nest?
Sooner or later, when he wants, he comes home.
I will boast to him of what I have found.

Rereading Shakespeare

Caesar crashed
at Pompey's pedestal:
or a spattered tissue, crushed
at the base of a park statue,
itself rubbed out by fog.
Speechless tongues
oozing volumes,
conspirators like trees.

The reports come in from home—
you rip up family photographs
in your agony. Faithless wife,
traitor son. I remember
when we visited the woman
who had burned her husband's face
from every slide, from Christmas,
birthdays, a scorched zero
displaying successions of babies.

It took me years of scrutiny
to place him at the picnic
with that woman, beside my mother and you,
all by the brook in swimsuits, cooking
and smiling from the early pages
of our own family album, before the revolts.

It must have been his face
(the statue in the fog;
the warrior rubbed out for good)
the man on the screen without a face
across from your biggest
photographic smile on record—
the young uniformed soldier

World's Fair trylon and perisphere
pinned to your shoulder.

How long would I be in coming
with the knife my love demands?
How long until you'd slash
your divine appearances
from our album life, how long
before occasions for photography
diminished, your image smashed forever?

I remember that trip—the woman
and her daughters. How
behind family jokes
of what a cute match we made
her blonde one
gave me erections
in the snow outside,
speaking of where
arrowheads might be found.

Far From the War

Four helicopters shot down by the Communists
appear on our pillow.

It is snowing.

Small windows in the wreckages
are slowly rinsed by frost.

We must arrange our heads
in a position that will leave them
undisturbed

all through the night

The Ex-Poet

Wondering is a typical pastime of the leisure class.
So Mao says,
The wondering about other minds
The wondering if the exterior world exists.

So:
I am reading *The Dialectics of Growing Peanuts*
and another useful book
The Dialectics of Bus-Driving,
the first written
by the successful director
of a North China peanut farm,
the second by Shanghai's
most decorated public servant.

So I won't lag behind
the development of objective reality.
The secret police.

Comrade, I urge you to do the same.
Be like our leader:
Think of the peanut field
shaking in warm July winds.
Begin to construct in your mind
a system of public transportation
flawless as a scientifically-grown peanut!
These are the important things in life,
not the shriveled peanut of philosophy . . .
Without direction the daydream
may be likened to a man who plants peanuts
under the seats of city buses—
and that is a madman!

No more time to compare the wind!
Take the imagination away from the water!
I personally wasted most of my life
scribbling about a woman I lost,
living in a future where we'd meet
one day by chance, the past
crushing the present of my pitiful life!

Puh!
Now all I'm interested in is how effectively I can cut this
    board
in two pieces: the philosophy
of the saw, the theory of the nail
that holds my world in place.

Summer Madness

A dragonfly plows into the wall of a grape

SOME JAPANESE POEMS
ABOUT ROY ROGERS

Introduction by Koichi K. O'Hara

Translated by Bill Zavatsky

*The translator dedicates these versions to Ron Padgett,
who read them and offered several important suggestions*

INTRODUCTION

There is something Japanese in our American homes.

And the Japanese psyche, Americanized past mere terrorism by Hiroshima and Nagasaki, has been filling with images of sixguns, cattle-drives, shootouts, hard-riding and -roping, and the plethora of cowboyiana called the Wild West almost before the wind over the deck of the U.S.S. Missouri had dried the defeated Nisei signatures. I myself have seen, in my own Tokyo home, broadcasts of the well-known horse-opera series *Bonanza* dubbed in the Japanese language, huge Hoss squeaking like a *sumo* wrestler who has stepped on a stray rowel.

American movies hit postwar Japan like a 3-D technicolor Hokusai wave. Tim Holt, Lash LaRue, Bob Steele of the eternally wounded left arm, the Cisco Kid and his Faithful Indian Companion, Hopalong Cassidy like a midnight dream of silver and snow—but nothing quite the like of Mr. Roy Rogers, "The King of the Cowboys," with his "Wonder Horse" Trigger, and the woman who would become his real life wife, Dale "The Queen of the West" Evans. The Roy Rogers phenomenon in Japan can be spoken of only in adjectives applicable to other 20th Century magical acts: the Disney Kingdoms, the McDonald's Burger, Teenage Car Culture, and more. There was once a removable pair of mouse ears in every American home.

But as cowpokes strummed and shot their way deeper into the Japanese mind, strange images combined. The *hototogisu* (nightingale) haiku-breath, sweet as Buddha's nostril but drunk with space and stumbling, embraced the mythical gunslinger of the Pecos. As evidence, read Mr.

Zavatsky's splendid translation of the haikus by Goto, Shabo, Itoki, Bojonju, and Onamoto. Here we find the "Wonder Horse" compared to a snowflake. And Harira's oddly beautiful pillow-song (another traditional genre) rides tall in the saddle of the new spirit.

And lest we drown in the lush blossom-jabber of Kuzaiman's "Song of Dale," Johnny Do is here to shake a mad-eyed beatnik fist in our face. Further, evidence, if any more were needed, of Japan's cultural up-to-dateness! Fortunately in Mamoru Shinohara's touching ode to Dale Evans we possess a more naive if not less sophisticated sensibility that tips the cherry blossom into the bell of a brand new tenor saxophone.

I would like to commend the diligence and skill of the translator, whose short-wave radio knowledge of the language does not seem to have hindered him from presenting us not only with wonderful poems, but with a living round-up of cross-cultural literary anthropology. The fair trade agreement with the West that has brought our Samurai epics and martial arts into the American household has been returned in kind!

KOICHI K. O'HARA

Autumn wind:
Everything I see
Is Roy Rogers.*

       Washi Goto

A snowflake
Alighting gently,
The Horse of Wonder, Trigger

       Wabata Shabo

The first who falls asleep
Is very fast
To be as Roy!

       Anonymous Senryu bedtime
       poem for children

Outlaws before cornflakes
He says, and out he goes,
This Roy Rogers.

       Sunamatsu Itoki

*Note: Goto soon repudiated this as a "false satori" poem, and revised the last lines to read: "Everything I see / Is not Roy Rogers."

Posse: "Did you hear it?"
"Hear it?" says Roy,
"I have eaten it!"

        Bonju Bojonju

What a delight it is,
When on the bamboo matting
In my grass-thatched hut,
All on my own,
I Roy-Rogers.

        Tachibana Fufuki

Nowadays even Trigger
Stomps and grunts,
Wanting his mojoonji suit!*

        "Ike" Onamoto

"Is she sound asleep?"—
This I ask the pillow.
"Yes yes," the pillow say,
"So put on your cowboy suit."

        Ara Harira

---

*Note: From the courting ritual where, in this attire of glass and turtle feet, a crab is set before the wooer.

SONG OF DALE

Tang blossom-apples my willow-air.
Irrational-wind trembles my bonnet to Noh-sense.
For this wind I have waited to explode
The petals of my fireworks-heart on the lake
Whose green-edge we, My Lord, did gallop-yodel.

Now I undo all my hair.
Now I unclip my spur-star.
Now the orange coocoo-peck-noise traps the day.

    Meija Kuzaiman

OPPOSITION

In my youth
I was opposed to school.
And now, again,
I'm opposed to work.

Above all it is health
And Roy Rogers that I hate the most.

Of course I'm opposed to the "Japanese spirit."
And human feelings and Dale Evans make me vomit!

I'm against any cowboys anywhere.
Kiss my *busai* you poets that write of them!*

        Johnny Do

*Note: *busai*: An untranslatable obscenity, actually a combination of the Japanese written characters signifying male, female, dog, and bean-sprout genital and excretory organs, all in a leprous condition. ("Do" is in reality Sonso Sonoso, an intellectual turned gas station attendant living in Tokyo. His pen-name is an attempt to further bolster his nihilistic, pseudo-"Beat" philosophy.)

TO THE QUEEN OF THE COWBOY KING

Whoa, Miss Evan how are you doll?
Do you remember Japan in Autumn?
How about Autumn in Nikko—
our big famous shrine outside Tokyo?
I mean, we have this saying, here goes:
"Don't say 'kekko' before you see Nikko"—
Dig me doll?
'Cuz "kekko" means "nice" or "pyjamas" . . .
like you on your hot-dog cowboy pony!
Miss Evan are you now in New York Times Square
part of your ranch of the big country
America, separated from Japan by Pacific Ocean Blue?
My name is Mamoru Shinohara.
I am a junior at the mechanical-college engineering.
Do you know the baseball game?
I am cool on the mound!
And do you know Mt. Fuji?
My home is near Mt. Fuji.
Mt. Fuji covered in snow
Is very beautiful, with comparisons toward you!
Snow now is in moon fashion
On the cliffs, like one thousand stampede cattle horns.
When I play saxophone with my group The Monsters
I think you here Doll!
Mt. Fuji is the symbol of Japan
and the comfort of my and our mind
I think. So is the cherry-blossom.
When I go to your pictures
it is like I am in your pictures.
I close my eyes, I put
the cherry blossom on your rodeo-hat,
I replace the silver guns
of Mr. Rogers with blossom also

I hope you do not mind, or he—
Mr. Rogers, The King of the West!
So get with it Doll
(Are you seventeen?) I am OK
U.S.-style
Waiting here by the sea
for your answer and picture if possible!

        Mamoru Shinohara

My New Year's Literary Resolutions

I'm casting a glance
at the idiotic statue
of my Complete Works,
elbows, knuckles, noses
of everything I've written.
And I'm sharpening
my hammer and my saw.

Now some of you have read
a few of the old style things
I've written through the years,
and maybe you'd give me
an argument, but
if I argued a little harder
then harder than that
each time you raised an objection,
pretty soon
you'd find yourself nodding your head
agreeing "Yes, Bill, your stuff stinks!"

And that is what I treasure
in a friend: the ability
to shut up
when threatened with physical violence.
But I'm not going to hurt you.
I'm not even going to
"lean on you a little"
like the image of a gangster.
My Jimmy Cagney impression stinks, too.
(My Dracula is great, however)

Though I'm not here
to suck your blood.
I'm here to announce

the opening of a new period
in my life as a poet!

Before I do, let me tell you
a bit about myself.
I don't like sports. I do like
the "highlights" however.
And my one sports fantasy
involves how fast I'd move
and what I'd do
among athletes gobbling along
in the slow-motion reality
of instant playback.
This isn't hard to visualize
and I think you can do it.

I make a point
of your being able to see
what I'm talking about
because my first resolution
has to do with *clarity*.
More than anything
in the coming year
I plan to *Be Clear*.

Let me illustrate.
I like to yank the pin
on the technicolor grenade
of metaphor.
However, this explodes
on contact, charring my lips.
The Latin poet Vergil
is responsible, whom I studied
in my youthful daze
"smeared with clotted gore."
From him dates my proclivity

for "aureate diction"
(a technical term
described below):
a problem like flashes
of silver on gold
in the classical cloud
in my head.

Yes I love that writing
so impossible to sustain!
Insisting on the autographs of the leaves
and fingerprints squeezed from waves!
This mode of expression
is like stations only radios
owned by Negroes can pick up,
and I don't have one.
So in the coming year
I will cease to be Vergilian
but probably remain
something of an aureate bum,
glorious hobo wading through
silvery puddles making a silk
suck when I trudge away
in stolen panties
from the line of some rich Mrs.

Clear as a postal scale—
that's how I'll be!
Clear as a fairy tale,
though as complex in idiocy!

Next the problem of revision.
A poet, as you know, likes
to "work over" his gems
until they blind with beauty.
Psychology tells us this

impulse is nothing less
than the wish to maim or kill.
The face of a parent
is etched like a target
on every poet psyche!
Pens are clearly weapons
or substitute penises:
an arrow for the boys,
a dick for the ladies.
Writing is nothing more
than axe-murder in glee
spattered over innocent
sheets of paper!
Thus, since revision is to suicide
as Tarzan is to ecology,
I don't plan to revise much
in the coming year, both
out of self-esteem (it hurts)
and brotherly love (it hurts you).

> (It seemed to me when I started this
> it would be much shorter!
> Not "more to the point"
> just a lot less. Yet
> how flushed I am with eager acceptance
> at these first fruits of my non-revisionist stance!

Let me confess it: I've been an unhappy man!
Unhappy in a million ways you couldn't understand . . .
What to do with three promising lines
scribbled ecstatically in a fresh blue
and white Columbia University notebook in 1965?
In fact the only thing written in that notebook,
part of why I flunked out . . .
I have dozens of such books,
all blank!

Then the Literary Market Place.
How to "break into print"?—forceps? dynamite?
Blow my way to the top?
Or something nobody's tried before . . .
"Print my work at once or I will kill you!"
"Take this literary gazette to Cuba at once!"
"Do not call the police; I am holding your wife . . ."

Deep dilemmas: What to do with words
like "shadowproof" that seem projected
through my brain from the wrapped mouth
of some shriveled Egyptian princess?
(More pastel shrapnel from that grenade)
shadowproof   shadowproof
(how to make the incision, remove the shadows)

And Reality: beating its fat shoe
on the face of the world—
Here's a girl with a ruby ring big as a siren on her finger . . .
Or the way Mars leans near the Earth whispering
    "bye-bye" . . .
Here in the country, a picnic, the band relaxed on the
    oom-pah grass:
a bumblebee testing the mouthpiece of a slide trombone . . .
An 84 year old maitre d' one evening on the train
who insatiably relives his life's greatest moment:
leaping out of a second floor bedroom window without
    pants
as he clutches my lapels, just along for the ride . . .
Insoluable conundrums day by day:
the potato chip company next to the auto-crushing yard . . .
problems problems problems!

Can I "make it" with a name like "Zavatsky"?
And what does *Zavatsky* mean?
Bananahead? Baby-of-the-Lightning? Actual Size?

Lobotomized-by-Sunshine? The Weeping Silencer?

Maybe another of my resolutions
ought to be to find a streamlined moniker
before another year rolls around . . .

As a matter of fact
I hereby resolve to legally change my name
to "_____" or "_____" or
       "_____"
or all three.
Anything you read by these poets
beginning January 1st
will actually be by me.
This is my final New Year's resolution,
and a noble act of faith in the future, too.

So there you have it:
Clarity, Anti-Revisionism, New Secret Identities.
Blasting away the old stylistic vanities
that held us apart, My Reader, My Love!
Such are my shining New Year's Resolutions:
for a work of art must raise problems, but give solutions.

Lessons

1.

"I am going away"
said the little *a*
of *they are*, "but
I will leave
a marker
to remind you
other letters
I was here.
There," he said
and hung it
in the air
like a tiny seed
between the *y* and *r*

2.

Go to sleep.
(me too)

When the two of us
are asleep
we'll build a ship
in the sink
drop by drop

Where we sail
I don't know.
Maybe to a land of snow
Maybe a star or two

Testament

A lot of times I've thought about suicide
No kidding
but then I worried about who'd find the mess
poor loving wife mangled with grief
pussycats climbing the walls, never the same
neurotic friend passing by who "just dropped in"
Ha! Some surprise!
I thought about who'd have to clean "it" up
blood all over typewriter keys
hair smeared to windowshades, 1/2 tongue in teacup
other tongue fragment drooling among Ko-Rec-Type
brain dangling outside in tree like broken glider
smashed by high velocity futility
eyeball discovered months later clogging vacuum cleaner . . .

I've pondered my changes for a mythology . . .
Too silly a life for Sylvia Plath-type gothic hubbub
Serious enough not to merit *profundo* Ogden Nash
    requiem
No exciting alter ego, no zippy pennames
little published barely known
oddball to famous critics
shining dumbbell even to closest friends

   . . . a skeleton of a poet
big plans   bigdeal blueprints scribbled in hot air . . .

Then suddenly it hit me
how
in a magnanimous gesture toward the future
I could will my scrap-flashes of genius
those whiffs of the eternal fracturing light
that I scribbled madly on pads and envelopes and

       matchbook covers
bequeath them to some other struggling mind
heavy on the willpower
Somebody who can fit these bits and pieces together
into great masterpieces of literature
after I blow my brains out

What about
"Slit open the wind and let me kiss my breath"
(one of my better lines, I think)?
Or how about one of my best titles
"Moonlight and Spies"
—to which I never could attach
the weird faces of words.
Then there's my one-word poem masterpiece
(unjustly neglected, I feel):
"pinosceros."

Yes
maybe some tender policeman-poet
faking a timesheet this very moment
to steal time to write a poem
could do with a helping hand . . .

And that great looker
in the giant shoes,
lipstick blazing around her smile
like an arsonist?

Or that popeyed anarchist there,
or that brilliant ten year old?

Imagine someone sad and crushed
armed with my bequest
expressing all the madness of the world
for free!

Yes
some goofy genius
maybe right now lurking in my old home town
bumping into a parking meter
stunned
my lawyer's letter trembling in his hands,
strong new glasses on . . .

A mind who at last will write my Zavatsky-Iliads . . .

Zavatsky-Iliads
Hmmmmm . . .

Just a minute while I write that down!

Goodbye

Headwinds as usual.

My myth now rests on the shores of the Pacific.

Water searches blue into distance.

The sea is spotted with freakish islands. A parachute would not help the Pacific the way it is falling down the sky.

Two things I wanted to do: touch the minarets with my hands going by in the air; fly like a germ, a letter in any word, on a newspaper page abandoned from the moon and sucked across space over America. Once I did cut a cloud over Natchez in two. A lonely boy in Kansas tilted the orange beak of his ballcap and jumped up and down in visionary furor. Seeing me. In Boulder a baby will never be the same. I have been seen, thousands of feet over bending shoulders of mother. At twelve the child is inscrutable. Beauty in shells, beauty in fractured facing of glass, beauty in stirring tissue. Inconsolable. At fifteen the child smashes its fist against one parent's mouth. Again, the curving eddy of blood reminds of something I have been.

Attitude.   Altitude.

The blood unravels. The child hangs and extends the thread of scarlet toward murder and light. And in light and dusk I travel, and am mine. And it is half in Pacific surf, half on a wormy rock of sea that you shall find me, faded, dammed inside the original letter of the word my signal is, my life, my time.

Real Bullets

This gun is beautiful.
Because the sky made it
and put it in my hand.

The moment I lift it
I know I'm going to shoot it.
But what am I going to use for real bullets?

And for targets, the construction
of real things. From where I stand
the task of sounds. The trees

twisted in their own self-archery,
the wind as it releases them
to fall, the nature of the rehearsal

philosophy steered by a million caterpillars
and wings and suns, the chainsaw
with its cranky industrious nibble . . .

. . . these children drifting by
I could murder so easily
after school, a mere formality . . .

But that would leave me cheated
by my own generosity. Again.
It's time to wave my lunch meat in the air,

time to be moving, a violent thing,
a monster examining each throat, inspecting
each cocoon through lightning,

marking each adam's apple lightly
with an X for a bullethole to be,
to be made by a real bullet . . .

2.

Perhaps this operation has gone too far?
Should I cut here? Should my finger be pressing that?
Maybe I'm losing my mind . . .

Didn't I graduate with honors?
Was I the one who could explain the nerves
to a child? Should I have kept

my weapon collection intact?
the sleeping all day, the resultant invisibility,
invincibility, the ability to win by simply closing my eyes . . .

All I have left is this
so tangible gun. Weighed and tested
by its own dumb object-responsibility
to perform in the cage of this hand

to foment, to be pressured
and pressed, and finally
to issue its report, as lead as event.

Maybe I should run back to the corner of my tomb
insert my arrows in their slots
and resume my Sebastian pose . . .

These are such real arrows.
And if I can adjust this pin-up lamp
correctly
so the arrow-shadows ripple over my fat

like streaks of real blood,
I can flood my eyes
with memories of school again,
my star pupil mastery
of how to hurt in place.
I'll start at the beginning
like an immaculate nun bending
to see the Stations of the Cross
in a boy's mouth
my veils roaring
in pain's delirious window . . .

Then I'll carefully dial my telephone
force the receiver under my halo
and count the times it rings
as I scream the seconds along

kissing the newborn moments goodbye
as they brush my lips.
Like a fingerprint technician hard at work
in a delivery room, the scene of the crime

Next:
the trick
of catching the world
in my teeth

3.

A whirlpool rented stacks of rings
to marry me!
I'm like an escaped convict of sky sucked
straight up into the womb
of quicksand vacuum cleaner cunnilingus!
The fishhook up my ass
hangs from a cloud!

But I did intend to bring you something real . . .
just about now . . . live ammo
not pale blanks. Phenomena unlike
the need to fall asleep
repeating *Iwo Jima, Iwo Jima*
over an envelope. I mean this line
beginning on this page, successfully
robbing you of trees,

stuffing words in your jittery mouths
anti-vitamins   shadow-arrows   blank cartridges
You grown used to licking millions of shells
their slimy tenants eaten by waves a million years ago . . .

A slimy arthropod wails inside my skull.
You see the worm inside me
move in gestures I can't see.
You're the last witness to my reality!
And do I trust your testimony? Ridiculous.
I'd rather depend on a blot of lightning
its eyeshadow floating with vampires
my neck in slow motion, the collisions
rinsing my hair in movie light . . .
I'd rather contend with something my own size,

like this uncontrollable urge to masturbate
drifting against my penis like a leaf . . . like an elephant
fallen from the thighs of all the women
I imagine I need,
like a crazed verb teetering
on the ledge of a mouth
swept by police spotlights . . .

The sledgehammer dreamlips the psychotic nipple

That line seems absolutely flawless to me.
Like the ice that cradled me when I wrote it
like Alexander the Great on view in a block of ice!
Because it was lining my coffin,
lending the landscape an aura of snowflake-fingerprint . . .
the mirrors of it, I mean.

Wait a minute.
Time out in this funeral!
This tactical self-bombing of my face from a toy
    self-airplane.
I'm going to run across the street to the park
and check if the moon is still contending
with that streetlight. Because the attention
span is a horror movie. I'll be right back.

O moon! You are less easy to catch!
Like a goon on leave from Murder Incorporated.
And the moon and the glass dome are neck-and-neck,
though the street light garners extra points
by blazing all through the day
under certain urban conditions.
So I guess if we see it
as a kind of stand-in for real moonlight
(though the sun is out),
like real bullets in a Western movie
Cherokee corpses in a Calvary story
awaiting the rouge of sunset, the violet pencil
dusking-in above eyes—
then you could say the moon wins,
the way jets dip noticeably in the air after mealtime

4.

So hold on to that pair of eyebrow tweezers
from 1752, still grand for removing

those hairsized arrows that line the nostrils.
Keep one eye peeled for the mummies embalmed in
    piano keys
the sunset of my eyelid on your eyelid
creating the third eyelid that swims between us:
Aurora Borealis dancing hysterically in sunglasses
by the chemical dawn, cosmetics of skyline pollution . . .

You want to flip through my this-month's quota of
    monster books?
You want to help me try on a few poses
in my new wrestling magazine?
You heard about the killer baby cribs?

Here is my manuscript in tattoo, *Teethmarks of the
    Wind*.
I'd like you just to browse
this unpublished novel of mine, *Slaughter's Daughters*,
based on a Japanese verb wheel
and the answers to all the questions people ask lightning
immediately after they make its hit parade

How about if I read you my new long poem
Night Comes to the Toys of This World
in which I suggest that the hobby of scale model building
in tandem with an illustrated theory of celestial influence
can produce a really understandable TV repair manual,
and dare you not weep uncontrollably over my
    childhood?

I was going to give you a real experience.
Schematic diagrams. 25 different chassis designations.
Leaves so you could feel wings on your face, real bullets
dug from innocent bystanders, for touching.
How sports controls your life, with photos.
I don't have time to catalogue the terrors

of the comma: the gleaming hooks, the jettisoned
    foetuses.
Or the exclamation point:
its unique approach to bowling.
You shall never know
why the skull
of the question mark
drifts menacingly
above a disembodied cornea:
what it sees
what it refuses to see as it stares
into the void of your face . . .

Because behind that void
that basketball pebbled with stars
is the seeable me: another glandular ruin
from teenage adolescence, as opposed
to all the other phases of adolescence—
the front seat phase of adolescence
the unidentified senior citizen in the river phase of
    adolescence
where everyone threatens to creep away and die
and secretly does
and years later we smell their missing bodies
rushing our face as we carelessly open the yearbook . . .

Autobiography:
I came into this world and I have one pore
—of braille—
and in this pore
is a lens, an ambulance, and a navy.
There used to be a baby but I crossed out the baby.
At night I love to flash lanterns through the trees
or behind dances of human knees
whispering "chopsticks" and "lullaby" and "highschool
    reunion

Thinking of fingerprints as birthscars
brings back my self-control in the form of famous wars
that took place at the edge of my cheeks
when my eyes cut a place for themselves to stay
in my face.
Or to prey on my face.
Or to pray for my face—I'm never sure.

5.

I had a lot of mothers
they were always kissing me.
Now gravity is the only plastic surgeon I trust enough
to operate on my face in the dark.
Then I can crush "Goodnight, Mommy" between my
    teeth—
the mirrors, false nipples, erect eagles, freckle TV—
that whole igneous rainbow of metaphor
sprayed into millions of cubic yards
in poems I wrote on the move with a suicide knob . . .

And isn't it time for my nightly flight to Hollywood?
Comparative studies—erection dimensions,
the state of Marilyn Monroe's asshole . . . but why hurry?
One is never late for appointments
in the world of bodily decay.
Perhaps that's why we twins
don't come out in photographs anymore:
mystery guests of Being and Nothingness . . .

But it wasn't always like this.
Once I hid as recent apples cool apples really intent.
I developed the striking power of my words.
All I had to do was see

YOUNG CALIFORNIA GIRL ARRESTED IN CAPITOL BLAST

and I was smearing stage blood on flashcube sites
seeking fuck like a concert rapist
in the sudden fingery light . . .

Then I suppressed my love for years
to seek a single artistic effect,
like "sunset (in) wrist" "traffic in diamonds"
    "doomwater root machine"
If I multiplied through by Pearl Harbor
and thought in plurals
It was possible to reconstruct the moment
of Princess Summerfallwinterspring's breath.
Others, love itself, would construct her death,
and my inventions are: mail order sheep and inflammable
    starlit erections.
I stared for days at figures moulded by supplementary
    lighting
finding death in space lyrical.
I wondered if you too found death in space lyrical
but I was too terrified to speak
as I studied the beam of moonlight caressing your rib,
like the ocean docked in a bedroom by a fingernail.

I wondered when your pulse would end its countdown
when I would lift slowly formally from the launching pad
into mammal moonlight
waving the technicians of your blood goodbye.
I wondered, "Which are the real bullets?" and I puzzled
over the intimate lightning between us—was it legible?
Observing a congress of bees in the brain of a rose
I decided that the movies aren't experience . . .
then bought my ticket and stumbled through the
    darkness

6.

And now as I load my gun
in this arena
flashing with images,
like one of the sighted who thinks only in braille . . .
Which are the real bullets
among shadow-arrows and mouthfuls of shadowfall?

I sit the weapon on the pillow next to me;
its cute little face hardly makes a dent.
And I find myself debating whether a bullet
fired into a mattress
creates a suitable vagina . . .

I rip off my snap-on rainbows
imagining I was the day
cut to pieces by rain.
My self-winding killer instinct seems to be running
Anti-personnel smile hardly smudged,
like a leftover party favor.
As I inject my for-fun dose of anti-poverty vaccine
that makes me rise and shine
sullenly I am aware that life is like music:
You die because they won't let you play
and if they let you play
you destroy yourself anyway

And thinking of what I promised you such a long time
    ago
like evolution
but failed to give,
I'm falling asleep
to be held by the hands in the air
to be passed along the geology of history
back through my snapshot as a smiling germ of the sea

forward through heaven, the angel part of my story
passed hand to hand through the air
to the flying saucer of sleep
in the cockpit egg of sleep
washed by the Am7 of waves
in the field recordings of sleep we know and hum
whose songnames we can never remember
like the name of a conspicuous star, the field
where we gained a conspicuous scar, the pain, the plan
the ship floating behind the bark of the tree
the cloudburst of countless individual fragments, real
    bullets
spinning from the sky, 16, I'm 16, I'm 31, I'm 182
shadow-arrows clustered around the faces in a cliff
a cliff a headboard on a bed: clams nails roses
under the eyelids of the censor, clutching a real bullet
in each hand, a foetus, a note for school, a rejection note
I'm dancing through everyone's bulletholes, history's
    bulletholes
the vagina created in pinewood by a bullethole
the bullethole created in the world by the vagina
dancing and singing through the bulletholes
into a real world
whose opposition I neutralize
by adopting its symbols,
                      my head
in a dream that makes my face at last beautiful
my feet walking the million cubic yards
splashing in the manslaughter of your blood, you
the one I did not know of
sleep
waiting in sleep, standing, falling sideways lips
pressed to the billowing faucet,
Egyptian, Etruscan, the eyebrows piling up
I'm going asleep
through the facial harp the rock masses

pushing a path a wave through sight seeing,
the ear footage, the rain-annexing hair, the handicraft the
    handicap
the badlands blue purple stormclouds
slipping through the bullethole silk
I'm going asleep . . .
          But all I seem to be doing
          is singing with my fabulous voice . . .

And maybe—

                And maybe it's about time—

And maybe it's about time I woke up screaming